Jesus Feeds the People

There was a boy who lived
in a land called Israel.

Dear Parent:

Your child's love of reading starts here!

Every child learns to read in a different way and at his or her own speed. Some go back and forth between reading levels and read favorite books again and again. Others read through each level in order. You can help your young reader improve and become more confident by encouraging his or her own interests and abilities. From books your child reads with you to the first books he or she reads alone, there are I Can Read Books for every stage of reading:

SHARED READING
Basic language, word repetition, and whimsical illustrations, ideal for sharing with your emergent reader

BEGINNING READING
Short sentences, familiar words, and simple concepts for children eager to read on their own

READING WITH HELP
Engaging stories, longer sentences, and language play for developing readers

READING ALONE
Complex plots, challenging vocabulary, and high-interest topics for the independent reader

I Can Read Books have introduced children to the joy of reading since 1957. Featuring award-winning authors and illustrators and a fabulous cast of beloved characters, I Can Read Books set the standard for beginning readers.

A lifetime of discovery begins with the magical words **"I Can Read!"**

Visit www.icanread.com for information on enriching your child's reading experience.

Visit www.zonderkidz.com/icanread for more faith-based I Can Read! titles from Zonderkidz.

How great your goodness is!
—Psalm 31:19

ZONDERKIDZ

Jesus Feeds the People

An I Can Read Book

Zonderkidz, 3950 Sparks Drive SE, Suite 101, Grand Rapids, Michigan 49546

Published in Grand Rapids, Michigan, by Zonderkidz. Zonderkidz is a registered trademark of The Zondervan Corporation, L.L.C., a wholly owned subsidiary of HarperCollins Christian Publishing, Inc.

Requests for information should be addressed to customercare@harpercollins.com.

Library of Congress Cataloging-in-Publication Data
Jesus feeds the people / illustrated by Kelly Pulley.
p. cm.
ISBN 978-0-310-71779-9 (softcover)
1. Feeding of the five thousand (Miracle)—Juvenile literature. I. Pulley, Kelly.
BT367.F4J47 2009
232.9'55—dc22 2008049731

Illustrated by Denis Alonso
Editor: Mary Hassinger
Art direction & design: Sarah Molegraaf

Printed in USA

25 26 /CMW/ 20 19 18 17

He heard about Jesus.
Jesus told people
about God's love.

The boy wanted to see Jesus.
So he got ready to go.
He packed a lunch
to take with him.

The boy's lunch had
five loaves of bread
and two tiny fish.
It was the right size lunch
for a boy.

The boy looked for Jesus.

He walked and walked.

“Where is Jesus?” the boy said.

The boy saw a boat in the sea.
Jesus and his helpers
were resting in the boat.
They were tired.

Jesus got out of the boat.
There were so many people.
They wanted to hear Jesus
tell them about God's love.

Jesus' helpers said,
"The people need food.
They are hungry!"

Jesus said, “We will
feed the people.
See if you can find some food.”

Jesus' helpers saw the boy.

He was holding his lunch.

They asked the boy,
"Will you share your lunch?"

The boy said,
"Yes! I will share my lunch."
Jesus' helpers took the boy
and his lunch to Jesus.

Jesus' helpers said,
"This is not enough food!
Eight months' pay
would not buy enough food
for this many people."
Jesus said, "Wait and see."

Jesus took the food.
He prayed and gave thanks
to God.
Then Jesus asked his helpers
to hand out the food.

It was a miracle!

The lunch grew!

There were many baskets
filled with food.

Five thousand people
ate a good dinner of
bread and fish that day.
Everyone was happy and full.

There was even food left over!
Jesus' helpers filled
twelve baskets with
the extra food.

The boy was very happy.
He loved Jesus very much.
He was so glad
he shared his food!